THIS JOURNAL BELONGS TO:

THANKFUL
TIMES
THREE

THE EASIEST
GRATITUDE
JOURNAL EVER

BY AMY SMYTH (AND YOU)

CHRONICLE BOOKS
SAN FRANCISCO

HELLO!

Whether you're new to gratitude-ing, or have some gratitude-ing experience, know that getting grateful is an excellent decision. Filling out *this* journal is an even better decision.

Research indicates that gratitude and humor help your brain, body, and relationships. It's actually quite shocking how much everything improves when you are gratefully laughing at life.

With each completed page in this journal, you'll get better at managing stress, boosting endorphins, improving your immune system, attracting and improving relationships, and becoming more optimistic, less materialistic, and more patient. Gratitude will enhance your life and make you a more pleasant person to be around; for that, everyone will be grateful.

This journal is devoid of corniness and long paragraph writing. It's low-pressure journaling. You write only three little things for each prompt whenever the mood strikes. Plus, this journal is undated. You can fill it out all in one day, once a day, once a week, or once every eight months. And if you've got gratitude coming out the kazoo, there's blank space throughout for freewriting, too.

Creating this journal has given me the opportunity to combine efficiency and humor, two of my favorite things, and the process has made me thankful times three for sure. I'm excited that we are on the same wavelength and that you appreciate a side of humor with your gratitude too. So, get in there, start fillin' stuff out, and let the gratitude and humor work their magic.

THREE CHALLENGES YOU OVERCAME THIS WEEK

1.

2.

3.

FOLDING HALF OF THE LAUNDRY IS A PERFECTLY LEGIT RESPONSE.

THREE OF THE BEST
THINGS ABOUT FRIDAY

1.

2.

3.

THREE PEOPLE WHO MAKE
YOU LAUGH CONSISTENTLY

1.

2.

3.

YOUR DOG COUNTS
AS A PERSON.

THREE TIMES YOU STUCK UP FOR YOURSELF

1.

2.

3.

THREE EXCITING WEEKEND
ACTIVITIES AHEAD

1.

2.

3.

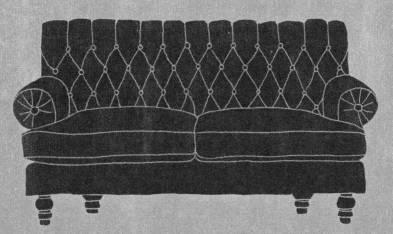

FALLING ASLEEP ON THE COUCH
WHILE PRETENDING TO WATCH
A MOVIE IS AN ACTIVITY.

THREE OF
THE BEST
SOUNDS

1.

2.

3.

THREE THINGS YOU SEE OUT THE WINDOW RIGHT NOW THAT YOU LIKE

1.

2.

3.

EVEN IF THERE IS
A DUMPSTER, FIND
BEAUTY IN THAT
DUMPSTER.

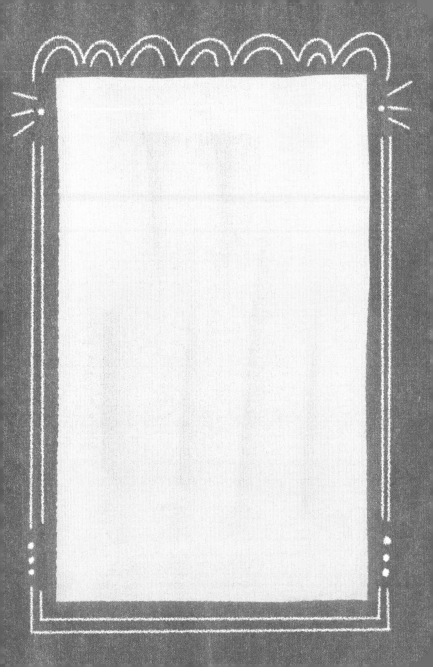

THREE WAYS YOU'VE GROWN

1.

2.

3.

THREE THINGS YOU'RE
LOOKING FORWARD TO

1.

2.

3.

NO MATTER HOW BIG OR SMALL

THREE TIMES YOU GOT "NO" FOR AN ANSWER THAT WERE CRUCIAL TO YOUR HAPPINESS

1.

2.

3.

THREE COMPLIMENTS
YOU'D LIKE TO GIVE

1.

2.

3.

**AIR CONDITIONER INVENTOR,
YOU'RE THE COOLEST GUY EVER.**

THREE THINGS THAT
SMELL SUPER GOOD

1.

2.

3.

NOW, GO SMELL THEM.

THREE SENTIMENTAL OBJECTS
YOU'VE SAVED AND WHY

1.

2.

3.

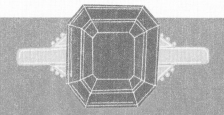

THREE ARTICLES OF CLOTHING
THAT LOOK GOOD ON YOU
AND ARE COMFORTABLE

1.

2.

3.

A COMBO WORTH COMMEMORATING

THREE BEST THINGS

ABOUT SLEEPING IN

1.

2.

3.

A BIT OF PRAISE FOR THE BED

THREE TIMES IT WAS
UNCOMFORTABLE TO
CONFRONT THE SITUATION

1.

2.

3.

CHANGE IS IN DISCOMFORT.

THREE APPROACHES TO ORGANIZING THAT HAVE MADE YOUR LIFE EASIER

1.

2.

3.

DONE

EVEN IF YOU
DON'T DO THEM
ALL THE TIME

THREE THINGS ABOUT NATURE
YOU CAN'T GET ENOUGH OF

1.

2.

3.

THREE THINGS YOU LIKE ABOUT CHORES

1.

2.

3.

IF YOU COME UP WITH THREE, YOU'RE A GRATITUDE PRO.

THREE OF THE
BEST GIFT-GIVERS
YOU KNOW

1.

2.

3.

THIS EXCEPTIONAL
TALENT NEEDS TO
BE CELEBRATED.

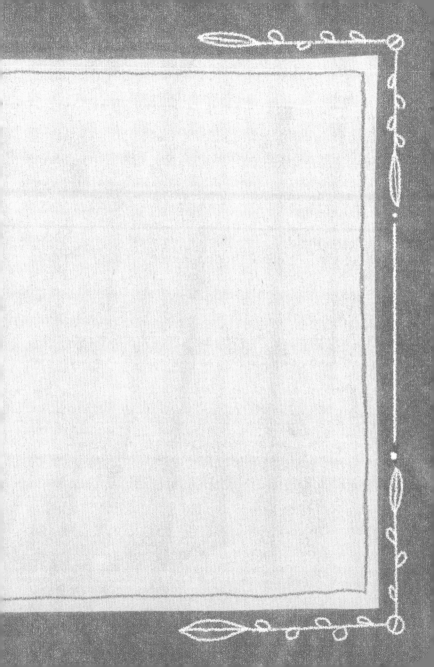

TOP THREE CONDIMENTS

1.

2.

3.

YOU COULD PUT THEM ON
YOUR SHOE, AND YOUR SHOE
WOULD TASTE GOOD.

THREE THINGS YOU DO TO LET
SOMEONE KNOW YOU LOVE THEM

1.

2.

3.

SPREADING LOVE

FEELS GOOD.

THREE THINGS YOU LIKE
ABOUT BEING HOT

1.

2.

3.

THREE COMBINATIONS OF FOOD
THAT ARE PERFECTION

1.

2.

3.

WEIRDER THE BETTER

THREE GREAT THINGS
ABOUT YOUR BRAIN

1.

2.

3.

EVEN IF IT'S NOT
GOOD AT MATH

THREE LIFE HACKS THAT
CHANGED YOU

1.

2.

3.

THREE WORK MOMENTS YOU'RE PROUD OF

1.

2.

3.

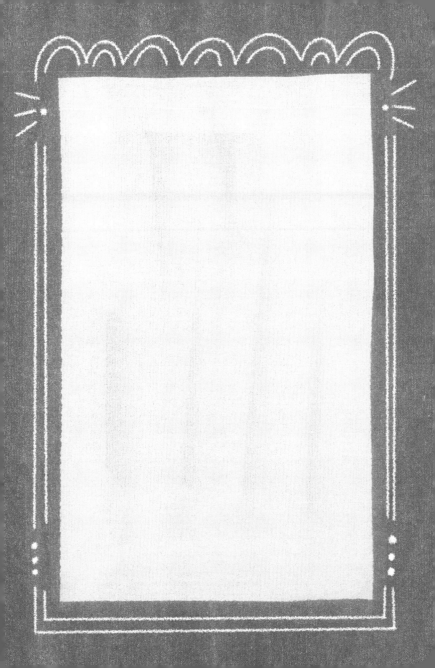

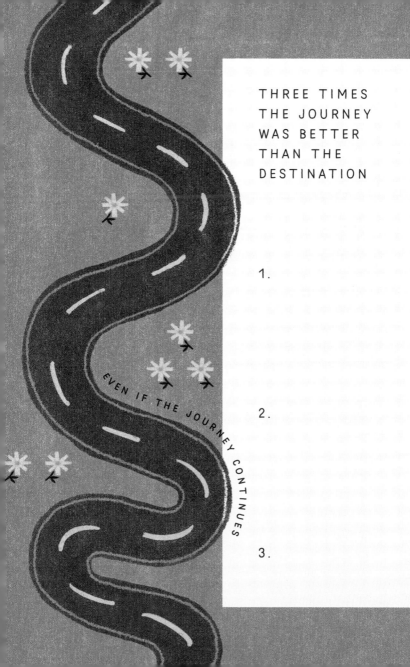

THREE TIMES
THE JOURNEY
WAS BETTER
THAN THE
DESTINATION

EVEN IF THE JOURNEY CONTINUES

1.

2.

3.

THREE HIGHLIGHTS OF THE DAY

1.

2.

3.

IF YOU GOT
HIGHLIGHTS,
HOW IRONIC.

THREE TIMES YOU WERE A BOSS

1.

2.

3.

THREE PEOPLE WHO WILL
LISTEN TO YOUR RAMBLINGS

1.

2.

3.

SEND EACH ONE A GRATITUDE TEXT.

THREE FAILURES
THAT WERE
THE SEEDS OF
SOMETHING
BETTER

1.

2.

3.

THREE THINGS THAT MAKE
YOU FEEL BETTER WHEN
THINGS ARE NOT GOING WELL

1.

2.

3.

LOOKING AT CAT
VIDEOS IS FAIR.

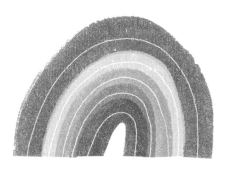

THREE DREAMS THAT CAME TRUE

1.

2.

3.

YOU MADE IT HAPPEN. YEAH, YOU DID.

THREE FOOD SMELLS THAT
MAKE LIFE BETTER

1.

2.

3.

NOW, TIME FOR
A SNACK.

THREE TIMES YOU'VE SURPRISED YOURSELF

1.

2.

3.

THREE OF THE SOFTEST
THINGS IN YOUR HOME

1.

2.

3.

LONG LIVE
SWEATPANTS.

THREE WAYS YOUR
BODY IS THE BEST

1.

2.

3.

EVEN IF IT DOESN'T ALWAYS COOPERATE

THREE THINGS YOU LOVE
ABOUT HARD WORK

1.

2.

3.

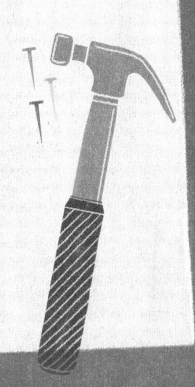

THREE TIMES YOUR
INSTINCTS WERE CORRECT

1.

2.

3.

**TRUST THE
PROCESS.**

THREE THINGS YOU
LOVE ABOUT EMAIL

1.

2.

3.

EVEN IF YOU HAVE MORE THAN 10,000
UNREAD MESSAGES, YOU CAN DO THIS.

THREE TIMES YOU SHOWED
GRACE UNDER PRESSURE

1.

2.

3.

CRYING IN THE BATHROOM AT
WORK COUNTS AS "GRACE."

THREE THINGS YOU COULD EAT DAILY

1.

2.

3.

THREE THINGS YOU LOVE
ABOUT YOUR FEET

1.

2.

3.

EMBRACE THE FUNKY TOE.

THREE EXPERIENCES
YOU LEARNED FROM

1.

2.

3.

SOMETIMES, ONCE IS PLENTY.

THREE FACES THAT YOU LOVE

1.

2.

3.

THEIR FACE INSTANTLY TAKES
YOU FROM GRUMPY TO HAPPY.

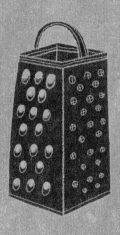

THREE WONDERFULLY EVERYDAY
THINGS YOU'RE GRATEFUL FOR

1.

2.

3.

THREE WAYS THE MOON
MAKES YOU HAPPY

1.

2.

3.

 IT'S A TIMELESS ICON.

THREE SONGS THAT
INSTANTLY CAUSE DANCING

1.

2.

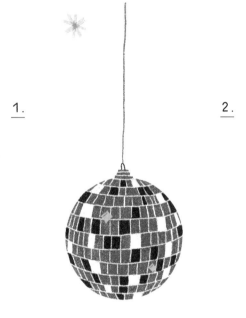

3.

EVEN IF IT ONLY HAPPENS IN YOUR CAR

THREE THINGS YOU LEARNED TODAY THAT YOU DIDN'T KNOW YESTERDAY

1.

2.

3.

WHAT FACTOID WILL ENTER
YOUR BRAIN TOMORROW?

THREE EMOTIONS YOU HAD TODAY THAT FELT GOOD

<u>1</u>.

<u>2</u>.

<u>3</u>.

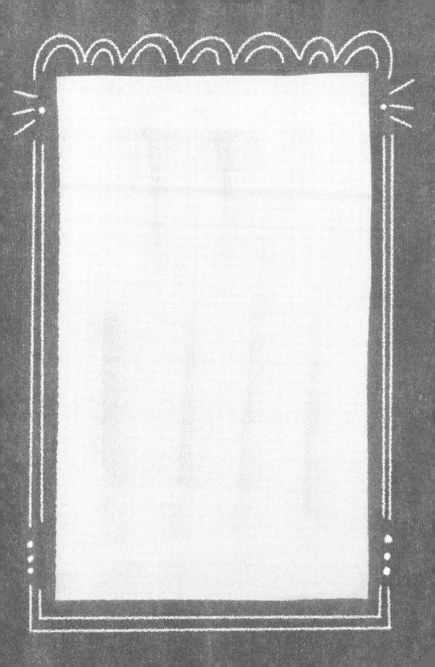

THREE LIFE DEVELOPMENTS
THAT SURPRISED YOU
IN A GOOD WAY

1.

2.

3.

SOMETIMES GOING OFF-SCRIPT IS THE
BEST THING THAT CAN HAPPEN.

THREE COMPLIMENTS YOU'D GIVE
TO DESSERT IF IT COULD HEAR

1.

2.

3.

DESSERT HAS BEEN
THERE FOR YOU. NOW BE
THERE FOR DESSERT.

THREE THINGS TO LOVE
ABOUT GRAY DAYS

1.

2.

3.

THREE THINGS THAT MAKE
GROCERY SHOPPING FUN

1.

2.

3.

RANDOM NEW SNACKS:

INTO THE CART YOU GO.

THREE THINGS THAT ARE
TOLERABLE ABOUT MONDAY

1.

2.

3.

YOU CAN DO THIS.

THREE CAREER GOALS
SET AND ACHIEVED

1.

2.

3.

THREE TIMES YOU WERE GLAD
YOU WERE A LITTLE NERDY

1.

2.

3.

THREE COLORS THAT
MAKE YOU HAPPY

1.

2.

3.

**COLOR RARELY
GETS THE RESPECT
IT DESERVES.**

THREE KITCHEN GADGETS THAT
IMPRESS YOU EVERY TIME

1.

2.

3.

IMAGINE PEELING CARROTS
WITH A KNIFE. OUCH.

THREE OF YOUR
FAVORITE BEVERAGES

1.

2.

3.

WINE IN A BOX COUNTS.

THREE TACTICS YOU USED
TODAY TO MANAGE STRESS

1.

2.

3.

EVEN IF THEY INVOLVED
UNHEALTHY SNACKS

THREE THINGS LOSS
HAS TAUGHT YOU

1.

2.

3.

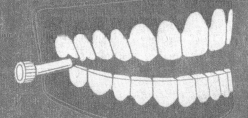

THREE THINGS YOU LOVE
ABOUT YOUR TEETH

1.

2.

3.

TEETH DON'T GET ENOUGH LOVE.

THREE RESTAURANTS THAT
NEVER DISAPPOINT

1.

2.

3.

COME BACK TO THIS
LIST WHEN YOU'RE TOO
HANGRY TO COOK.

THREE OF THE COZIEST
THINGS EVER

1.

2.

3.

**EVEN IF YOU LOOK LIKE A SMALL BEAR
WALKING AROUND IN YOUR ROBE**

THREE OF THE BEST THINGS
ABOUT BEING ALONE

1.

2.

3.

THREE PAST CRUSHES WHO MAKE YOU LAUGH NOW

1.

2.

3.

IF YOU'RE BLUSHING, THAT'S NORMAL.

THREE TEACHERS WHO
MADE YOU SMARTER

1.

2.

3.

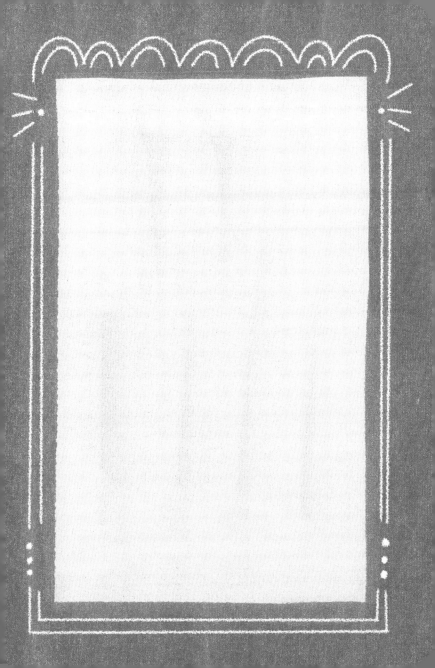

THREE PEOPLE YOU'D BE GOING
DOWN THE WRONG PATH WITHOUT

1.

2.

3.

GO AHEAD AND WRITE THEM
THANK-YOU NOTES.

HOME
SWEET
HOME

THREE THINGS YOU LIKE
ABOUT WHERE YOU LIVE

1.

2.

3.

ADMIT IT: YOUR WEIRD
NEIGHBOR IS AMUSING.

THREE THINGS YOU'RE GLAD
YOU DON'T DO ANYMORE

1.

2.

3.

THREE AREAS OF YOUR
HOME YOU LOVE

1.

2.

3.

THE BATHROOM CAN BE A
FIVE-STAR VACATION SPOT.

TOP THREE THINGS YOU'RE GRATEFUL FOR AT THIS VERY MOMENT

1.

2.

3.

THREE HEARTBREAKS THAT MADE YOU STRONGER

1.

2.

3.

EVEN IF IT
WAS A CRUSH
IN FIRST
GRADE

THREE THINGS YOU LIKE
ABOUT THE VOICEMAILS YOU
SAVED ON YOUR PHONE

1.

2.

3.

IF THEY ARE ALL FROM YOUR
MOM, APPRECIATE YOUR MOM.

THREE THINGS YOU LIKE
ABOUT BEING COLD

1.

2.

3.

THREE ANNUAL EVENTS
YOU LOOK FORWARD TO

1.

2.

3.

NO PENALTY IF YOU WRITE
PUMPKIN SPICE LATTE SEASON

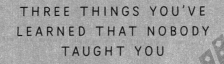

THREE THINGS YOU'VE LEARNED THAT NOBODY TAUGHT YOU

1.

2.

3.

THREE CHALLENGES YOU'RE
GRATEFUL FOR TODAY

1.

2.

3.

LIFE IS TOUGH, BUT LIFE DOESN'T
KNOW WHO IT'S DEALING WITH.

THREE THINGS THAT ARE
FUN ABOUT SUNDAY NIGHT

1.

2.

3.

YES, FUN

THREE ATTEMPTS AT SOMETHING
THAT DIDN'T WORK OUT

1.

2.

3.

THREE DISHES OTHER PEOPLE MAKE THAT ARE THE BEST

1.

2.

3.

LOVE IS THE SECRET INGREDIENT.

THREE EVERYDAY OBJECTS YOU'RE GRATEFUL FOR

1.

2.

3.

AND LET'S MAKE IT MORE CREATIVE THAN "MY PHONE."

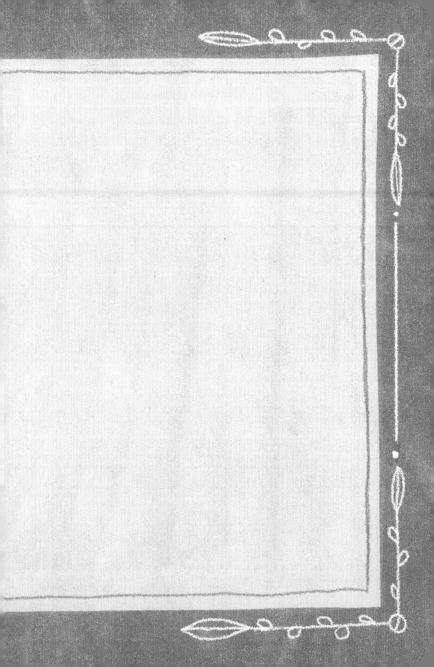

THREE FAVORITE PLACES FOR A NAP

1.

2.

3.

NAPPING APPRECIATION COULD
PROBABLY FILL THIS ENTIRE JOURNAL.

THREE THINGS YOU WANT
TO LIKE ABOUT EXERCISE

1.

2.

3.

EVEN IF ONE OF THEM
IS THAT IT'S A GOOD
EXCUSE TO WEAR YOGA
PANTS ALL THE TIME

THREE OPINIONS YOU'VE HAD THAT HAVE CHANGED WITH TIME

1.

2.

3.

TIME HEALS ALL OPINIONS.

SUMMER '02

THREE GOOD MEMORIES

1.

2.

3.

THREE THINGS PEOPLE DO
TO GAIN YOUR TRUST

1.

2.

3.

NOW TELL THESE PEOPLE
THEY'RE PRETTY GREAT.

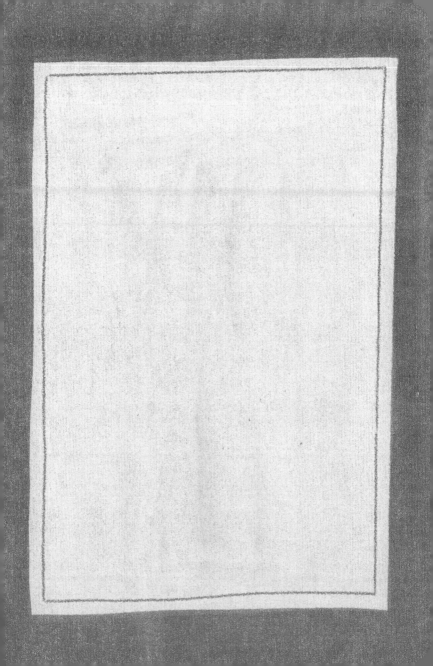

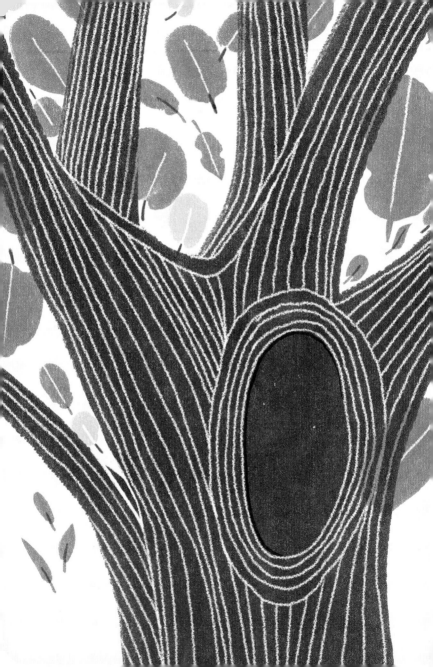

THREE THINGS YOU
LOVE ABOUT TREES

1.

2.

3.

**TAKE IT A STEP FURTHER
AND GO HUG ONE.**

THREE THINGS YOU'RE MOST GRATEFUL FOR RIGHT NOW— ANY THREE THINGS

1.

2.

3.

THREE TIMES YOU WERE RIGHT

1.

2.

3.

FOR THE RECORD, INTERNAL
GLOATING IS ACCEPTABLE.

THREE SONGS THAT REMIND YOU OF SOMEONE YOU LOVE

1.

2.

3.

THREE THINGS YOU LOVE ABOUT THE CLOTHES YOU ARE WEARING RIGHT NOW

1.

2.

3.

IF YOUR UNDERPANTS DON'T GIVE YOU A WEDGIE, CONSIDER YOURSELF FORTUNATE.

THREE THINGS THAT
RFLAX YOU BEFORE BED

1.

2.

3.

THIS IS A JUDGMENT-FREE ZONE.

THREE FRIENDS OR FAMILY
MEMBERS THAT KEEP YOU STRONG

1.

2.

3.

LAUGHING AT NOTHING IS
YOUR FAVORITE ACTIVITY.

TOP THREE DECISIONS
YOU'VE MADE

1.

2.

3.

THREE THINGS YOU LOVE
ABOUT YOUR KITCHEN

1.

2.

3.

SHOW SOME RESPECT FOR THE
ROOM WHERE THE FOOD IS KEPT.

???

THREE QUESTIONS THAT DON'T HAVE ANSWERS, AND YOU'RE HAPPY ABOUT IT

1.

2.

3.

AH, THE MYSTERIES OF LIFE

THREE REASONS YOU
APPRECIATE THIS JOURNAL

1.

2.

3.

GRATITUDE FOR THE GRATITUDE
IS VERY META.

THIS ONE IS FOR BOOTS.
WITHOUT HIM, THERE WOULD
BE NO SENSE OF HUMOR.
THANKFUL TIMES A MILLION.

Amy Smyth has been making a living designing,
illustrating, and writing since 2006. Her hobbies
include eating dessert, watching Philadelphia
sports, and making sarcastic comments.

ISBN 978-1-7972-2622-4

Manufactured in China.

MIX
Paper | Supporting
responsible forestry
FSC™ C136333

Design by Hillary Caudle.
Typeset in Mila Sans.

10 9 8 7 6 5 4 3 2 1

Chronicle Books LLC
680 Second Street
San Francisco, California 94107
www.chroniclebooks.com